W9-BYA-217

Pretty Princess PARTY

HIDDEN PICTURE PUZZLES

BY
JILL KALZ

ILLUSTRATED BY
JACK PULLAN AND LEN EPSTEIN

PICTURE WINDOW BOOKS
a capstone imprint

DESIGNER: LORI BYE
ART DIRECTOR: NATHAN GASSMAN
PRODUCTION SPECIALIST: KATHY MCCOLLEY
THE ILLUSTRATIONS IN THIS BOOK WERE CREATED DIGITALLY.

PICTURE WINDOW BOOKS
1710 ROE CREST DRIVE
NORTH MANKATO, MN 56003
WWW.CAPSTONEPUB.COM

LIBRARY OF CONGRESS CATALOGING-IN-PUBLICATION DATA
CATALOGING-IN-PUBLICATION INFORMATION IS ON FILE WITH THE LIBRARY OF CONGRESS.
ISBN 978-1-4048-7943-0 (LIBRARY BINDING)
ISBN 978-1-4048-8078-8 (PAPERBACK)
ISBN 978-1-4795-1886-9 (EBOOK PDF)

DIRECTIONS:

Look at the pictures and find the items on the lists. Not too tough, right? Not for a clever kid like you. But be warned: The first few puzzles are tricky. The next ones are even trickier. And the final puzzles are for the bravest seekers only. Good luck!

Printed in the United States of America in
North Mankato, Minnesota.
032013   007223CGF13

TABLE OF CONTENTS

Kingdom of Chills

- walrus
- owl
- fox
- hare
- lemming
- seal

4

5

Sweet Treats

- bicycle
- lizard
- beach ball
- Popsicle
- ice-cream cone
- scooter

Tea Party

11

Home, Sweet Home

- baseball
- motorcycle
- raccoon
- crow
- garbage can
- toad
- doll
- newspaper
- lawn mower

Treasure Chest

- bumblebee
- paintbrush
- lion
- fairy
- compass
- dragon
- elf
- skunk
- kite

Getting Pretty

- candle
- goldfish
- pony
- toothbrush
- cactus
- starfish
- chipmunk
- rose
- rainbow

Fancy Dance

- unicorn
- daisy
- purse
- teapot
- bowling ball
- spoon
- horseshoe
- paper doll
- kitten

Underwater Royals

- duck
- submarine
- watermelon
- turtle
- puffer fish
- soap
- anchor
- parrot
- map

21

ROYAL GRILL

Picnic Lunch

- dandelion
- fly
- jump rope
- duck
- dog
- coconut
- ant
- lantern
- French horn

23

Polo Practice

 gopher

 tire

 canary

 baseball

 tiger

 penguin

 salmon

 skate

 tennis racket

 ram

 bugle

 tulip

24

Hooray for Play!

 snail

 ladybug

 nest

 squirrel

 mouse

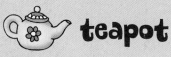 teapot

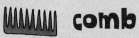 comb

 diamond

 caterpillar

 boat

 flower

 butterfly

Princesses on Parade

 coin

 sun

 necklace

sandcastle

 dragonfly

armadillo

star

piano

donkey

heart

scissors

toucan

28

Winged Jewels

 swan

 ladybug

 sheep

 chicken

 whale

 goose

 turkey

 camel

 panther

 goat

 coyote

 alligator

31

FOUND EVERYTHING?

Not quite! Flip back and see if you can find these sneaky items.

dolphin

goggles

tuba

strawberry

teddy bear

rolling pin

ladder

snow globe

Internet Sites

FactHound offers a safe, fun way to find Internet sites related to this book. All of the sites on FactHound have been researched by our staff.

Here's all you do:

Visit *www.facthound.com*

Type in this code: 9781404879430

Look for all the books in the series:

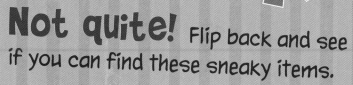

CHRISTMAS CHAOS

HALLOWEEN HIDE AND SEEK

OUT-OF-THIS-WORLD ALIENS

Pretty Princess PARTY

SCHOOL SHAKE-UP

ZOO HIDEOUT